NO WAY!

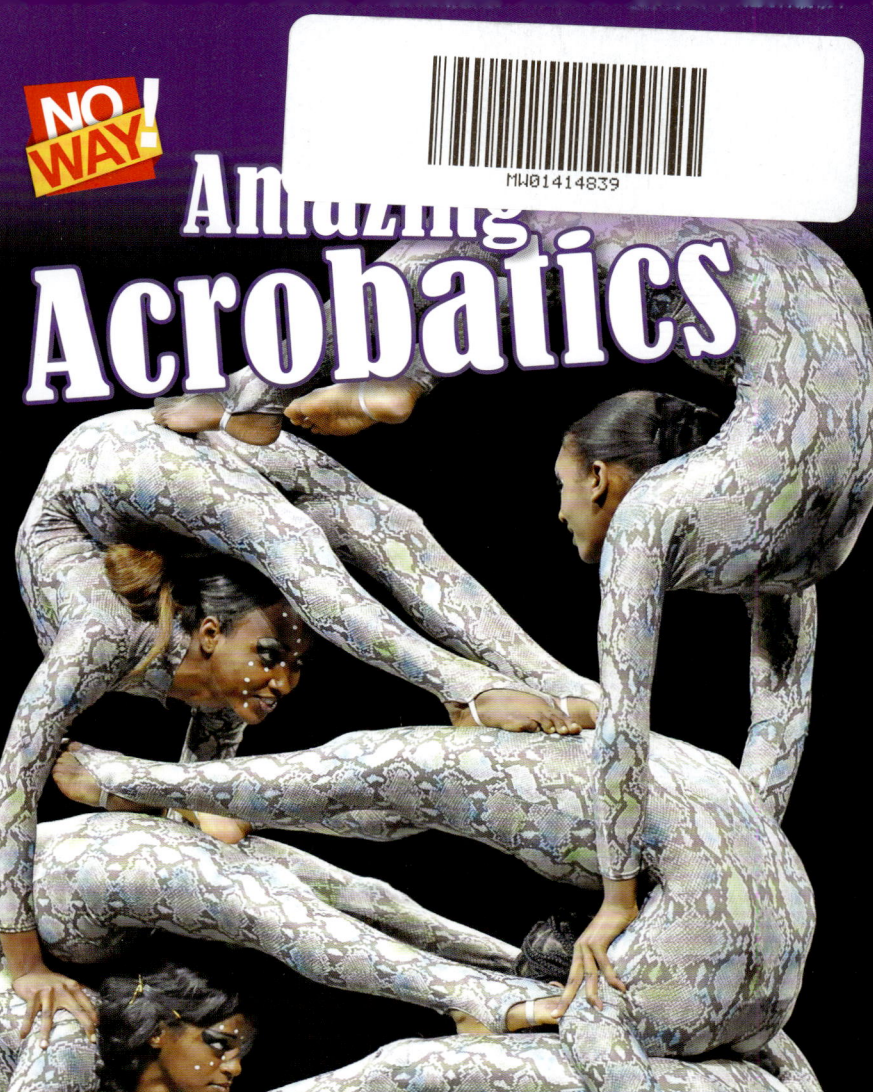

Amazing Acrobatics

Wendy Conklin, M.A.

Consultants

Timothy Rasinski, Ph.D.
Kent State University

Lori Oczkus, M.A.
Literacy Consultant

Publishing Credits

Rachelle Cracchiolo, M.S.Ed., *Publisher*
Conni Medina, M.A.Ed., *Managing Editor*
Dona Herweck Rice, *Series Developer*
Emily R. Smith, M.A.Ed., *Content Director*
Stephanie Bernard/Susan Daddis, M.A.Ed., *Editors*
Robin Erickson, *Senior Graphic Designer Designer*

The TIME logo is a registered trademark of TIME Inc. Used under license.

Image Credits: pp.4–5 Tim Boyles/Getty Images; p.8 Chien-min Chung/Getty Images; pp.12–13, 20–21, 26–27, 32 Illustrations by Timothy J. Bradley; p.14 Hulton Archive/Getty Images; p.15 New York Public Library Digital Collections; pp.16–17 Joseph Okpako/WireImage; pp.18–19 Jose R. Aguirre/Cover/Getty Images; p.24 Creative Commons Jumper 2 by Tony Hisgett used under CC BY 2.0; p.33 Wolfgang Kaehler/LightRocket via Getty Images; pp.34–35 Hemis/Alamy Stock Photo; p.36 Gaye Gerard/Getty Images; pp.36–37 Perry Mastrovito/Getty Images; pp.38–39 TORSTEN BLACKWOOD/AFP/Getty Images; pp.40–41 REUTERS/Natasha-Marie Brown; pp.42–43 The Register-Guard Eugene, Oregon; back cover Wolfgang Kaehler/LightRocket via Getty Images; all other images from iStock and/or Shutterstock.

Notes: Only people with the proper training should perform the various acrobatics and activities described in this book. The answers to the mathematics problems posed throughout the book are provided on page 48.

Library of Congress Cataloging-in-Publication Data

Names: Conklin, Wendy, author.
Title: No Way! Amazing Acrobatics / Wendy Conklin, M.A ; Consultants Timothy
  Rasinski, Ph.D. Kent State University, Lori Oczkus, M.A., Literacy
  Consultant.
Description: Huntington Beach, CA : Teacher Created Materials, [2017] |
  Includes index.
Identifiers: LCCN 2016026805 (print) | LCCN 2016038865 (ebook) | ISBN
  9781493836116 (pbk.) | ISBN 9781480757158 (eBook)
Subjects: LCSH: Acrobatics--Juvenile literature.
Classification: LCC GV552 .C66 2017 (print) | LCC GV552 (ebook) | **DDC**
  796.47/6--dc23
LC record available at https://lccn.loc.gov/2016026805

Teacher Created Materials

5301 Oceanus Drive
Huntington Beach, CA 92649-1030
http://www.tcmpub.com

ISBN 978-1-4938-3611-6
© 2017 Teacher Created Materials, Inc.
Printed in China WAI002

Table of Contents

The Art of Acrobatics. 4
Acrobatics from China 6
Basics of Balancing 10
The Birth of the Aerialist. 14
Parkour 22
Bending Over Backward 30
The Circus Under the Sun. 34
Let's Run Away to the Circus 42
Glossary 44
Index 45
Check It Out! 46
Try It! 47
About the Author 48

The Art of Acrobatics

Imagine walking on a cable more narrow than your foot across the expanse of the Grand Canyon—without a **tether**. Visualize swinging on a **trapeze** and somersaulting through the air before grabbing the next trapeze swinging toward you. How about riding a unicycle while juggling flaming hoops over your head? Acrobats have accomplished each of these **feats**.

Acrobatics is more than just flying through the air. It is the demonstration of flexibility, strength, balance, and coordination. The word *acrobat* comes from the Greek word *akrobatos*, meaning "walking on tiptoe." But acrobatics is more than just walking on a high wire. Today, acrobatics includes **parkour**, swinging on trapezes, juggling, riding unicycles, and more. Think of the **agility**, balance, and coordination required to accomplish these activities. That's what it takes to be an acrobat.

Acrobatics Everywhere!
You will find acrobatic elements in all kinds of sports. These include martial arts, gymnastics, ballet, and diving, to name just a few.

Is It a Sport or an Art?

Some people consider acrobatics to be a sport. Acrobats train and practice to achieve the motions and movements they master. Other people consider acrobatic feats an art for audiences to enjoy. The truth may be that acrobatics is both a sport *and* an artistic performance.

Acrobatics from China

Chairs and tables balance in the air as acrobats flip and catch them with their feet. They juggle bowls and jars, and they walk on tightropes. They call their performance "the show of a hundred tricks." Amazingly, acrobats performed these acts almost 2,000 years ago. The show did not actually have 100 tricks, but it did have a variety of daring deeds to watch.

For thousands of years, acrobatics has been alive and well among the Chinese. Long ago, **peasants** and laborers used common items such as jars, pitchforks, tables, and chairs to perform these stunts. Family members performed together, balancing bowls on their heads and on poles. Often, dance accompanied their exploits.

As time passed, the Chinese worked to perfect acrobatics. The Han dynasty in China spanned from 206 BC to AD 220. During that time, village festivals included handstands, somersaults, and other acrobatic tricks. They even incorporated music into their performances.

About 400 years later, the Tang dynasty ruled in China. At that time, acrobats performed shows at the imperial court, which included the emperor, his family, and other high-ranking officials. In one painted image from that time, a man balances a pole on his head while six people perform stunts on that pole.

The Very First Acrobats

People have been practicing acrobatics for thousands of years. The ancient Minoans (2000 BC) painted images and carved figurines that show acrobats leaping over the heads of bulls. Some historians think this is what they did during funerals.

Continuing the Tradition

Four spinning plates balance atop sticks in each hand while a performer stands on top of another performer's shoulders. An acrobat foot-juggles a large pot with a full-grown person inside. Unique lighting, costumes, and music work with the acrobats' movements to tell a story.

Welcome to a modern Chinese acrobatics show!

Acrobatics have been a part of Chinese culture for many years. Traditionally, skills such as foot-juggling, balancing, and flipping have been passed from generation to generation. Today, many families send their young children away to train with masters in acrobatic schools. Students live and train with **troupes**, enduring pain and hardships. Students from rural areas attend these schools in the hope for better lives. If they become stars, they can help provide for their families.

The acrobat masters are strict and expect students to work hard to perfect their routines. Acrobats must perform more daring, dangerous moves if they want to keep the audiences coming back for more.

Practice Makes Perfect

Acrobat masters say that one minute on stage is equal to 10 years of practice. This means that doing a difficult movement is not easy, even though it may appear that way. Acrobats spend years perfecting movements, flexibility, and balance so that it looks nearly effortless.

Basics of Balancing

An acrobat climbs on top of her partner's shoulders and then climbs the vertical ladder that balances on his head. Once she gets to the top of the ladder, she juggles several objects in the air while her partner below also juggles.

One by one, 10 performers climb aboard a bicycle, stacking their bodies side by side and one on top of the other. Incredibly, they balance as a driver rides the bicycle around the stage.

Another acrobat rides across a tightrope on a unicycle. His partner swings from a small platform that extends from the unicycle under the tightrope. Imagine the concentration needed to maintain balance.

What do those scenes have in common? They're all examples of balancing acts. Old drawings of multi-person balancing acts tell us that this art form is nothing new; it has been around for thousands of years. While these acrobats make the feats look easy, they take concentrated balance to accomplish them.

A Big Pyramid!

A common balancing act includes human pyramids. In Japan, 161 boys created a human pyramid! Now, think about a solid pyramid shape. What is the volume of a pyramid with the following measurements?

Base: 8 cm by 12 cm

Height of pyramid: 20 cm

Hint: $V = (\frac{1}{3}) Ah$; A is the area of the base, and h is the height.

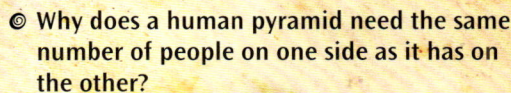

- Why does a human pyramid need the same number of people on one side as it has on the other?
- What might happen if a single person on a multi-person pyramid were to lean to one side?
- Why would it help a person in a human pyramid to extend her arms to either side of her body?

Staying Balanced

Physics plays a large role in how acrobats achieve balance. To keep from falling, an acrobat balancing on another performer must keep his or her center of mass (CoM) directly above that other performer and is usually located in the stomach area. The CoM is the balancing point of each performer. For example, each person in a human pyramid must maintain the position of his or her CoM to support the larger formation. If one performer leans forward or backward, the center of **gravity** shifts and the performers may fall.

Acrobats also use their limbs or other objects to help them stay balanced. If an acrobat only extends one arm while balancing on top of her partner, the torque caused by gravity can cause her to tip. By extending her other arm, she restores her balance. Performers can also use horizontal poles to keep their balance.

CoM

A

What Is Torque?

Acrobats need to understand torque, which is a force that can cause a performer to spin and lose balance. That's why they use both arms or poles to maintain their CoM.

The Birth of the Aerialist

While acrobats have performed for thousands of years, the flying trapeze was not introduced until 1859 in France. French acrobat Jules Léotard invented it. When he was a child, his job was to open the skylights over the pool in his father's gymnasium. To do this, he swung from rope to rope opening the windows. Over time, Léotard mastered this swing and invented what we know today as the *flying trapeze*. On November 12, 1859, Léotard became a performer.

Poles on the Tightrope

To keep their balance, many tightrope walkers hold long horizontal poles that are bent slightly. These poles might be weighted at both ends. When an unexpected gust of wind comes along, acrobats use the poles to counter that wind and stay balanced. The poles also help them keep their CoM directly over the rope.

That same year, a man named Emile Blondin walked across Niagara Falls on a tightrope as more than 5,000 people watched in amazement. As time went on, Blondin included theatrical elements in his tightrope walks. He dressed as an ape and pushed a wheelbarrow for one of his acts. For another act, he blindfolded himself, carried a man on his back, and stopped halfway through the walk to cook an omelet. Audiences could not believe their eyes.

Both Léotard and Blondin were aerialists. An aerialist is an acrobat who performs in the air.

The Invention of the Leotard

The **leotard** is named after Jules Léotard. He thought that the original outfit created for his performances was too bulky. So he asked for something to be made that fit tightly, and the leotard was born.

Just Swingin'

Aerialists adjust the lengths of their trapezes depending on how far and how fast they need to travel. The trapeze acts as a large **pendulum**. It swings the aerialist back and forth. The pendulum hangs from a fixed point, or **pivot**. When aerialists swing from trapezes, they become weights for the pendulums. Sometimes, aerialists swing from one trapeze to another trapeze. They may perform **rotations** in the air before catching the second trapeze. Or other aerialists swinging from different trapezes may catch them in midair. If two aerialists work together in a performance, they must time their swings perfectly.

Shape of a Trapeze Swing

A trapeze swings in the formation of an arc as it completes a period. As the aerialist adds more momentum, the arc becomes longer. When an aerialist slows down, the arc becomes shorter.

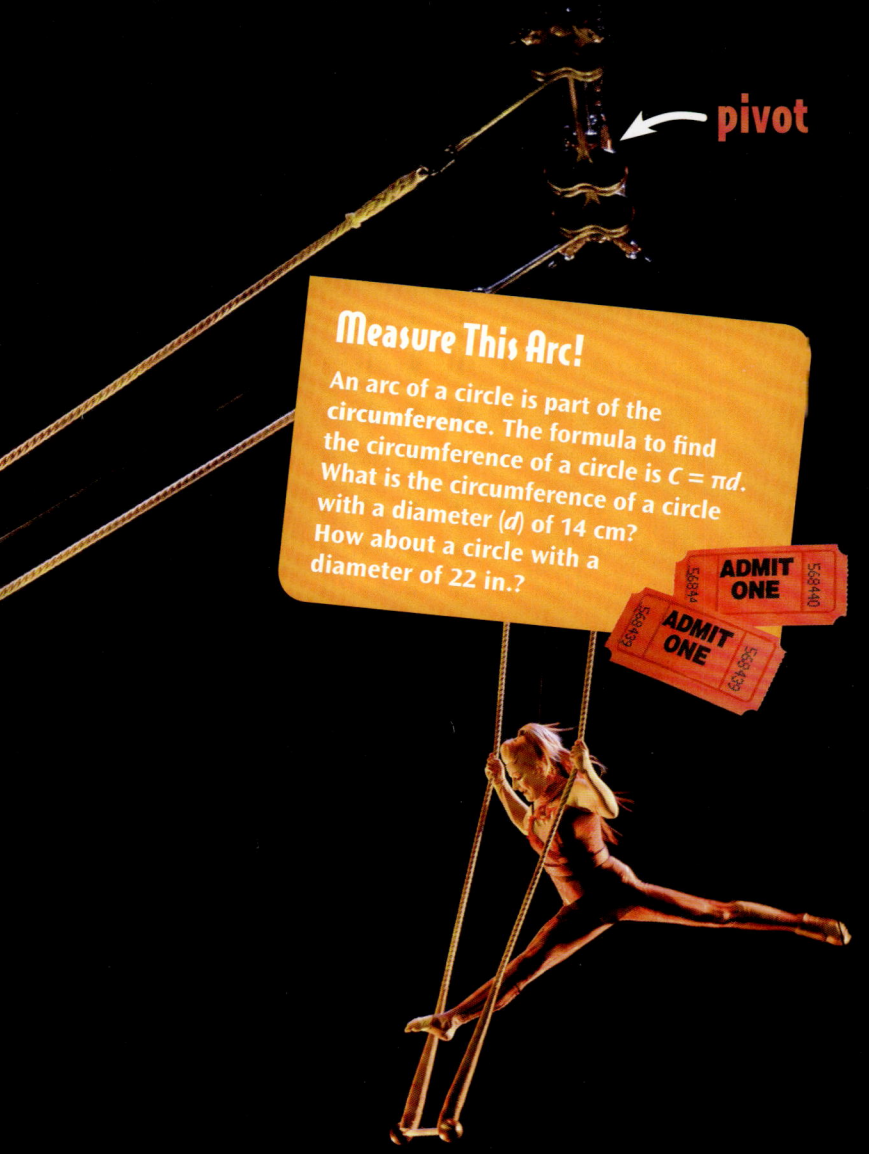

Measure This Arc!

An arc of a circle is part of the circumference. The formula to find the circumference of a circle is $C = \pi d$. What is the circumference of a circle with a diameter (d) of 14 cm? How about a circle with a diameter of 22 in.?

The length of time it takes the pendulum to swing from one position back to the starting position is the period. If the trapeze is long, the period will also be long. In contrast, if the length of the trapeze is short, the period will also be short.

Flippin' Out

As an aerialist swings from trapeze to trapeze, she rotates her body in the air before her partner catches her while hanging from another trapeze. To rotate faster in the air, an aerialist tucks in her arms and legs. This movement conserves energy and creates more momentum. On the other hand, an aerialist may want to do only one flip in the air. So, she **elongates** her body to make the flip last longer.

Getting More Air Time

Two or three Russian barres can be attached to create more lift for the aerialist. This greater flexibility allows for higher jumps and more rotations in the air, if desired.

Somersault Names

The types of jumps that aerialists perform are the same jumps gymnasts do. Some of these jumps include *double twisting double*, *triple sault*, and *triple twisting double*.

The Russian barre is a flexible 13-foot (4-meter) pole, similar to a tightrope, on which an aerialist performs stunts. Two **porters**, one on either end, hold the barre horizontally. The aerialist uses the barre like a balance beam and a trampoline combined. Together, the porters can help the aerialist bounce on the barre to gain momentum to jump into the air. While in the air, the aerialist can flip and rotate her body. Just as on the trapeze, an aerialist can decide how fast she wants her body to rotate. She does this by either tucking in her feet and arms or extending her body.

- How might attaching two to three Russian barres end to end provide more lift for an aerialist?
- How does tucking in or elongating the body relate to an aerialist's speed?
- What conclusions can you draw about someone who wants to become an aerialist?

DIG DEEPER!

Daredevil Flyers

Aerialists must trust their partners as they jump from trapezes to their partners' hands 45 feet (13.7 meters) above the ground.

The aerialist swings to gain momentum and lets go of the trapeze in midair.

An aerialist brings in his legs and arms close so he can rotate at a fast pace.

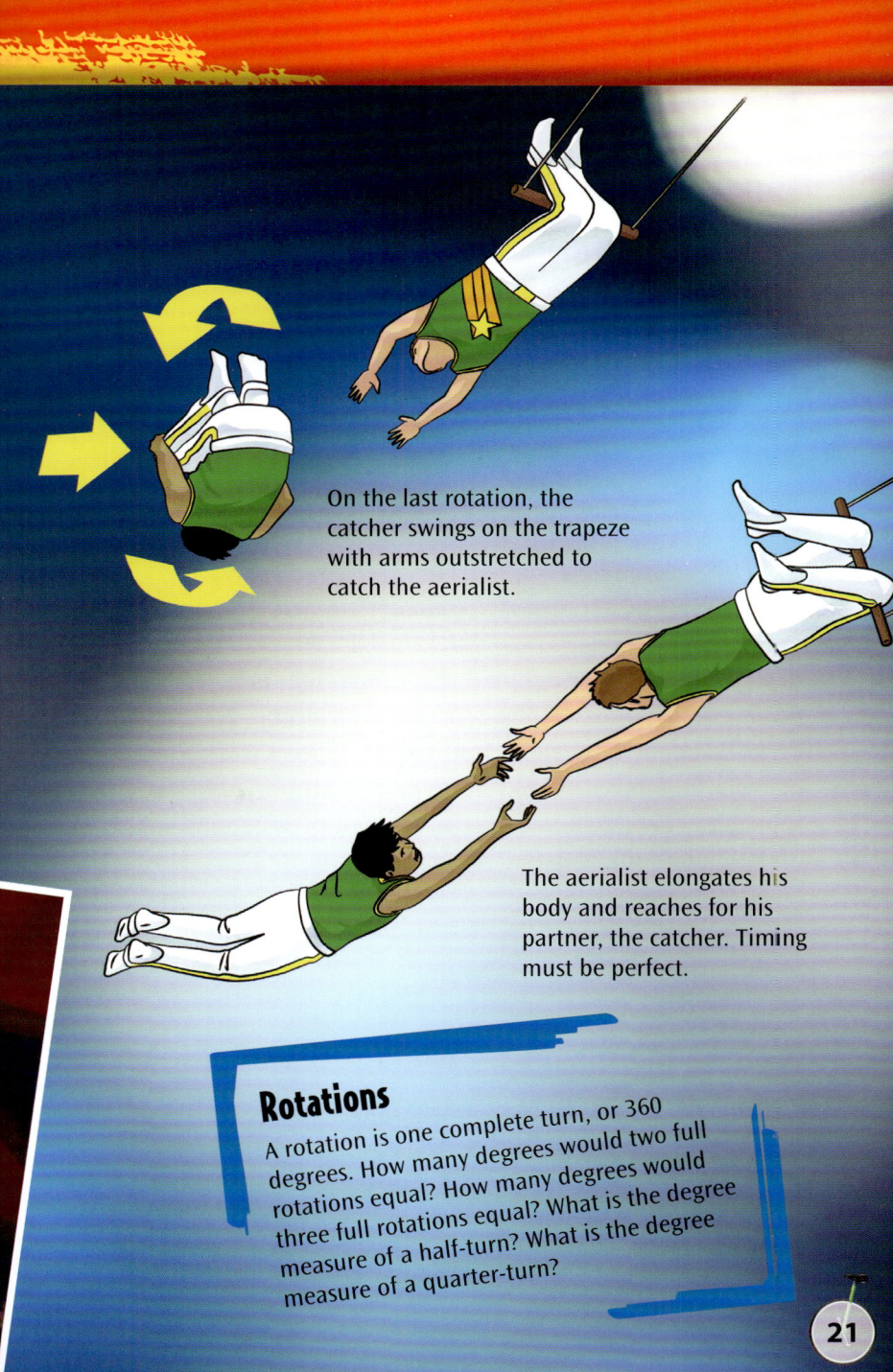

On the last rotation, the catcher swings on the trapeze with arms outstretched to catch the aerialist.

The aerialist elongates his body and reaches for his partner, the catcher. Timing must be perfect.

Rotations

A rotation is one complete turn, or 360 degrees. How many degrees would two full rotations equal? How many degrees would three full rotations equal? What is the degree measure of a half-turn? What is the degree measure of a quarter-turn?

Parkour

For people who do parkour, the world is nothing but an obstacle course. Why stroll down the sidewalk when they can jump from building to building, swing through windows, and land in a ground roll only to jump up again and keep going? They climb buildings with ease, slide down roofs, and grab ropes, swinging from place to place. This is no movie stunt, although it may seem like one. Each jump is performed with extreme precision and care. They move with the environment, using their skills and the world around them to get from one place to another in the most efficient manner.

This sport is also called *freerunning*, the *art of movement*, and the *art of displacement*. Some people refer to this as an intense sport, but others say it's an art or, a **discipline**. Parkour evolved from movements taught in the French military's obstacle course training, focusing on balance, agility, and coordination. Those who practice parkour say that it takes courage, dedication, and strength to master. These athletes are always improving and taking on new challenges.

On TV and in the Movies

If you have seen the latest action movies, then chances are you've seen parkour in action. Films such as *Casino Royale* and *The Bourne Legacy* use the movements that parkour teaches to outrun the "bad guys."

What Do You Call Them?

Athletes who practice gymnastics are called *gymnasts*. Acrobats are people who perform acrobatics. So, what do you call people who practice parkour? These extreme athletes are called *traceurs*.

The Philosophy Behind Parkour

Although it is difficult to pinpoint exactly when parkour first began, most people say it has its origins in the 1980s in France. There, a group of young men began practicing the art of displacement among the urban landscape. They called their group *Yamakasi*, meaning "strong man and strong spirit." Those young men honed the craft of parkour, including jumps, climbs, vaults, and rolls.

A Dangerous Sport

When the first parkour videos were released to the public, many people began trying the movements without proper training. Unfortunately, two youths in France died making jumps. This led to an emphasis on safety. People who practice this sport must do it in safe environments. It's best to learn the discipline of the sport instead of taking uncalculated risks.

Learning Parkour in School

In some inner-city schools and community sports centers in the United States, parkour is being taught to kids. And the interest in such classes is spreading quickly. Parkour coaches take specialized trainings. There are courses and classes in certain cities that anyone, including adults, can take to learn the movements.

Believe it or not, parkour does not encourage risk-taking. Those who seek rushes of **adrenaline** are not encouraged to participate in this sport. Instead, parkour encourages traceurs to develop their minds and bodies while also mastering their movements. In their minds, traceurs work to overcome fear and inhibition. With their bodies, they practice movements over and over. In this way, they can manage risk and perform the movements safely.

Parkour comes from the French word *parcour*, which means "course." Traceurs see the world as one large obstacle course. They reject the way society expects people to move around in these spaces. Instead, tree branches, rocks, railings, and buildings are only obstacles for them to maneuver around in a more fluid manner.

Parkour Obstacle Course

There are many different ways to move through an environment. Traceurs want to move in the most efficient, fluid manner possible. Consider the example below. The traceur can choose at least four different routes. The distance is not necessarily the same for each. Specific jumps shorten the route in some cases but might take more energy out of the traceur. Which route is the most efficient? Why?

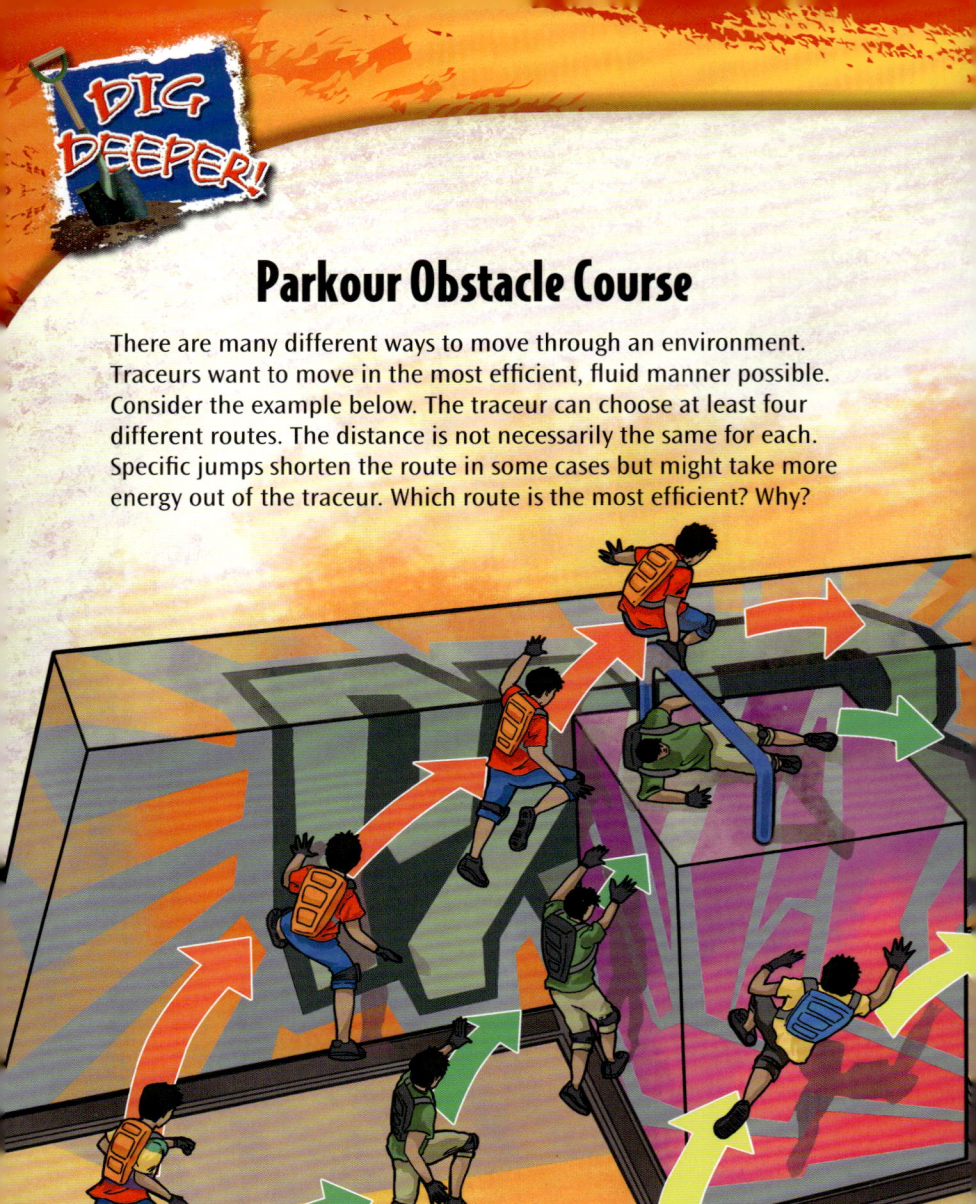

How They Parkour Their Way Around

To perform parkour, traceurs need exceptional upper body strength, so they often spend a lot of time working out and maintaining physically fit, lean bodies. Through their movements, they develop incredible grip strength. This enables them to grab onto buildings and other objects.

Precision is key in parkour. Making a good estimation for how to navigate a course is not good enough, nor is it safe. Traceurs sometimes train for months before making new jumps. For example, let's say a traceur wants to jump across two buildings that are four stories tall. That is about 30 feet (9 meters) high! The jump spans 9 feet (2.74 meters) between the two buildings. The traceur begins by jumping that distance at a lower height, such as 6 feet (1.8 meters) from the ground, which is less risky. He may spend months mastering this jump, but once he masters it, he knows that he can perform it at any height.

Traceurs train in groups and perform drills similar to the game Follow the Leader. The leader swings on a railing and lands in a roll, and the others copy the same movements.

Female Freerunner

Luci Romberg is a professional freerunner and stuntwoman. She has appeared in movies such as *Ghostbusters* (the reboot) and *Captain Fantastic*. Her television credits include *NCIS* and *Criminal Minds*. In 2014, she won the Taurus World Stunt Award for Best Overall Stunt as the stunt double for actress Melissa McCarthy in the film *Identity Thief*.

STOP! THINK...

A traceur is able to jump 2 feet high and 6 feet across. There are some obstacles on her path. Which of these obstacles will the traceur be able to jump over or across?

A. a park bench that is 1 yard tall and 2 yards wide
B. a planter that is 24 inches tall and 36 inches long
C. a recycling bin that is 36 inches tall and 3 feet long.

6 feet

2 feet

Bending Over Backward

Their bodies easily twist and fold into shapes like pretzels. Graceful movements help them transition from backbends into splits and then into handstands. They climb on top of one another and appear to have super-human strength. As they perform push-ups, their feet curl over their heads. It looks so easy, and yet it is so difficult. These performers, known as **contortionists**, do mesmerizing tricks with their bodies.

Contortionism is a performance art that requires discipline, focus, effort, and patience. These athletes' goals are to show the beauty of the human body. The acts tell stories through beautiful movements.

Bend like a Yogi

Contortionists perform many stretches similar to ones done in yoga classes. These stretches help the body to maintain flexibility. Some people say it helps keep them young as they age.

Elastic Man

Alexey Goloborodka was born in Tula, Russia, in 1994 and began performing at about the age of five. He is trained in contortionism, classical dance, and martial arts. The combinations of movements from these disciplines makes for a graceful, effortless performance.

Where Did Contortionism Begin?

Contortionism has been around for hundreds of years. Mongolians made it into an art form, and in 1941, the Mongolian State Circus was started. This introduced a wider audience to contortionists for the first time. The performances showed the importance of strength, balance, and flexibility. Since then, many contortionists come from Mongolia. There, children aspiring to be contortionists attend special contortion schools. Coaches specialize in this art form. Many contortionists go on to become professional circus performers.

Why Can't You Be More Flexible?

It takes extensive training to do what contortionists do. Typically, professional contortionists begin training at just five years old. In the beginning, they train for two or three hours a day, six days a week, teaching their bodies to be flexible. Even outside the gym, they continue to practice and stretch to gain more flexibility.

It takes years for ligaments and muscles to lengthen so that the joints become mobile. As contortionists work toward these goals, they become more flexible and can perform more movements.

Strange Ideas

There are many myths that surround contortionism. Some people think that contortionists are born with double-jointed spines, which means their spines are especially flexible. Others think that as babies, they were soaked in bone-softening chemicals.

Compared to others, contortionists tend to have very straight spines while standing. When bending, their spines extend beyond a typical person's spine. It is common to find that at least one parent of a contortionist is extremely flexible. This suggests that there could be a genetic connection to this skill.

While most people will never become professionals, with a coach's help, almost anyone can practice contortionism. This art form is gaining popularity. Today, contortion classes are found in major cities around the world.

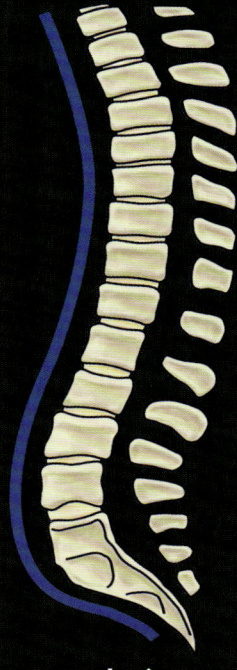

normal spine

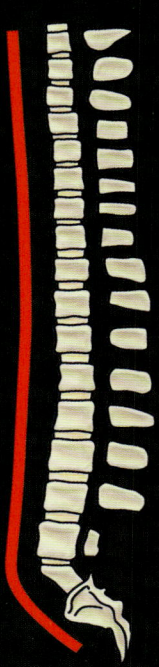

contortionist's spine

The Circus Under the Sun

What does a person who is an athlete, entertainer, and storyteller do for a job? Join the circus, of course! There is one circus that is more prestigious than all the rest. It is Cirque du Soleil. There, you will find aerialists performing on trapezes. Contortionists work together to build pyramids using their strength and flexibility. Clowns prance around making people laugh. The only things missing in this circus are the animals.

Back in the 1980s, Cirque du Soleil had its beginnings in Quebec, Canada, with just 20 street performers. They walked on stilts and performed life-sized puppet shows. Over the years, the show developed and grew in popularity. Today, it combines theater performance and circus skills and is the largest performing company in the world, with about 1,300 performers.

Cirque du Soleil troupes come from a variety of athletic backgrounds. These include gymnastics, synchronized swimming, diving, and martial arts. Some former Olympians have joined Cirque du Soleil once their competitive days are over. Agility and fitness are advantages for auditioning to be in one of the shows.

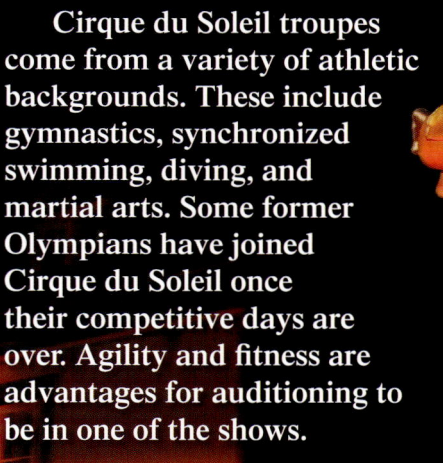

In the Beginning

In 1984, Guy Laliberté, Cirque du Soleil's founder, saw the 450-year anniversary of the discovery of Canada as a way to promote his performers and shows. He booked a tour across Canada's provinces. He named it Cirque du Soleil because *soleil* means "sun," and "the sun symbolizes youth, energy, and strength."

The Chance to Be a Performer

Hundreds of would-be performers show up in hopes of joining Cirque du Soleil. The tryouts are rigorous and last for weeks. Coaches choose only a few to continue the training. However, these trainees have no guarantee that they will ever be part of a Cirque du Soleil performance. They compete to be part of the database of performers that Cirque du Soleil calls upon when they need new performers.

The Wheel of Death

One act in Cirque du Soleil is the Wheel of Death. A large wheel rotates while performers walk in and around two attached hoops. Sometimes, performers even do flips inside the hoops as the wheel turns!

During their second round of tryouts, these hopefuls take intense classes that not only develop their athletic abilities but also their performance skills. For example, they attend voice and acting classes. They practice **improv** and dancing, since these are both parts of Cirque du Soleil acts. These classes help them make the important transition from competitive athletes to performers. If they cannot master the new skills, then they do not make the cut. After six grueling weeks of training, only a handful of athletes are selected for the database.

Cirque du Soleil tent in Montreal, Canada

Centering the Big Top

When putting up the tent for the performance, the center of the big top cannot lean by even a millimeter. If the center is off by one millimeter, then the backside of the tent will be off by half a meter. The school attached to the tent will be off by one meter. And the kitchen, which is next to the school, will be off by a few meters.

Tricks of the Trade

In Cirque du Soleil, the high-flying aerialists perform on Russian swings. A Russian swing contains a platform that is suspended from a horizontal bar with steel rods. The acrobats stand on the platform and pump it so that it swings. With enough swing, the platform can make 360-degree rotations around the horizontal bar. The acrobat is looking for just the right arc to jump. The swing creates a **centrifugal force** so the acrobat can jump with enough altitude to flip in the air.

Not only do acrobats need to swing and flip, but they also must do these tricks wearing costumes. These costumes include hats, wigs, and beards. If beards weigh too much, they can affect acrobats' performances. Wigs that are too heavy may throw off the **equilibriums** of the artists. Costume designers have to think about the right materials and designs so that the acrobats can swing successfully. They carefully design hats that won't obstruct the acrobats' visions. After learning to swing successfully, the acrobats practice in full costume so they can make the necessary adjustments in their swings and flips.

Keeping the Trainees Safe

As the performers train on the Russian swing, the window of error has to be small to keep them safe. Trainers don't want their trainees getting hurt. In fact, these aerialists wear safety harnesses at all times while training.

Weighty Matters

A wig can weigh different amounts, but a 14-inch wig made from human hair weighs approximately 6 ounces. A costume can weigh 2 pounds. An average baseball cap weighs 4 ounces. In all, approximately how much extra weight in pounds and ounces would a performer carry while wearing these items? If a performer's weight plus the weight of these costume items must not exceed 130 pounds, what is the weight limit of the performer?

Balancing but Not on a High Wire

Not all balancing acts performed by Cirque du Soleil are on high wires. Acrobats also balance their bodies on Chinese poles. Chinese poles are vertical poles ranging from 10 to 30 feet (3 to 9 meters) tall and 2 to 3 inches (5 to 8 centimeters) in diameter. Acrobats use only friction and muscle power to climb to the tops of Chinese poles. Once they climb, they use grip strength to hold themselves in place.

One of the most difficult movements is the flag, which requires tremendous core and upper body strength. In this movement, performers hold on with their hands and extend their bodies horizontally as if they were flags waving in the wind. Performers use reverse handgrips with their thumbs pointing to the ground. Their top arms pull while their bottom arms push to balance the forces behind this move.

Being off by the slightest millimeter in a hand position or a leg position makes all the difference in how the performers appear to the audience. That's why those selected to be in Cirque du Soleil are the best of the best.

Finding Talent

Cirque du Soleil has the largest casting department in the world. Scouts are always on the lookout for athletes, actors, and singers who all play parts in the shows. They look for performers who possess artistry, athleticism, and showmanship.

41

Let's Run Away to the Circus

Modern-day acrobatics pushes trainers and performers to take on new challenges. Today's audiences want to be given good shows—they want to be mesmerized. So, acrobats must practice for hours, days, months, even *years* to condition their bodies to perform amazing feats.

The next time you watch an incredible acrobat or consider joining the circus, think about the preparation behind the performance. Envision yourself swinging from a trapeze or bending your body into a pretzel. Appreciate the balance, coordination, discipline, and hours of practice. Working toward perfection relies on lots of practice. That's what it takes to perform extreme acrobatics. So, do you have what it takes?

Changing All the Time

Many people believe that animals in circuses are often mistreated. Because of this, some circuses no longer include animal tricks. Cirque du Soleil is one of the circuses that excludes animals.

Do You Want to Join the Circus?

To be part of circus acts today, you might want to take gymnastics, acting, and dance classes. Being an athlete is key to performing the difficult stunts, while knowing how to dance and act will help you to be prepared for circus showmanship.

Facinet Sylla, former circus performer, is a talented acrobat and dancer originally from Conakry, Guinea, in Africa.

Glossary

adrenaline—a hormone released when frightened, excited, or angered that speeds up heart rate and increases blood flow

agility—the ability to move quickly and easily

centrifugal force—a force that seems to move a person away from the center while going in a circular motion

circumference—the distance around a circle

contortionists—people who can move their bodies into unusual shapes

discipline—an exercise that trains a person in a skill

elongates—stretches one's body as far as it can in length

equilibriums—states of being physically balanced

feats—great accomplishments

gravity—the force that pulls individuals and objects toward the center of Earth

improv—the act of performing as one goes along, without preparation

leotard—a tight-fitting outfit made from spandex and used in acrobatic performances

momentum—the act of gaining speed, forward motion, and active force

parkour—freerunning; the art of running, leaping, and climbing quickly and efficiently

peasants—poor people

pendulum—something that is suspended from a fixed point and moves back and forth

physics—the study of matter, energy, force, and motion

pivot—the fixed point that a pendulum (such as a trapeze swing) hangs from

porters—strong acrobats who assist in lifting, launching, carrying, etc. other members of an acrobatic troupe

rotations—circular turns; full rotations measure 360 degrees

tether—a rope or a chain that is fastened to a person to keep him or her safe from falling

trapeze—a short bar that hangs from a high point for an acrobatics performance

troupes—groups of actors, singers, or acrobats who perform together

Index

aerialists, 14–16, 18–21, 34, 38
Blondin, Emile, 15
Bourne Legacy, The, 22
Casino Royale, 22
center of mass (CoM), 12–14
China, 6, 8
Chinese poles, 40
Cirque du Soleil, 34–38, 40, 42
contortionists, 30–34
foot-juggling, 8
Goloborodka, Alexey, 30
Han dynasty, 6
Japan, 11
Laliberté, Guy, 35
leotard, 15
Léotard, Jules, 14–15
Minoans, 6
Mongolia, 31
Mongolian State Circus, 31
Montreal, Canada, 37
parkour, 4, 22–26, 28–29
physics, 12
Quebec, 34
Russian barre, 18–19
Russian swing, 38
Tang dynasty, 6
torque, 12
traceurs, 23, 25–26, 28–29
Wheel of Death, 36
Yamakasi, 24
yoga, 30

Check It Out!

Books

Barnaby, Hannah. 2013. *Wonder Show*. HMH Books for Young Readers.

Blume, Michael. 2013. *Acrobatics for Children and Teenagers: From the Basics to the Spectacular Human Balance Figures*. Meyer & Meyer Fachverlag und Buchhandel GmbH.

Jones, Jason. 2015. *Parkour: The Complete Guide to Parkour and Freerunning for Beginners*. CreateSpace Independent Publishing Platform.

McLemore, Anna-Marie. 2015. *The Weight of Feathers*. Thomas Dunne Book for St. Martin's Griffin.

Ormand, Kate. 2015. *The Wanderers*. Sky Pony Express.

Simon, Linda. 2014. *The Greatest Show on Earth*. Reaktion Books.

Videos

Cirque du Soleil. *The Concert*. Cirque du Soleil.

National Geographic Channel/Jayashree Panjabi and Max Quinn. *China Circus: Elites*.

Websites

Parkour.com. *The Official Website of Parkour*. http://parkour.com/.

Try It!

Imagine that you have been hired to design a new acrobatics show. You need to incorporate as many different styles as possible to thrill and entertain audiences so that they keep coming back. Innovation and creativity are important as you brainstorm answers to the following questions.

- What types of acrobatic performers will you need for your act?
- What types of equipment will be needed for your performance?
- Will there be a theme for your performance?
- What will you feature as your main attraction?

About the Author

Wendy Conklin has spent the last 15 years honing her skills as a writer for both teachers and students. She is always looking for ways to be creative in both her writing and in the things she chooses to do in her everyday life. She lives with the belief that the secret to being creative is to put oneself in situations of learning new skills, so now she spends much of her time learning upholstering, drawing, and playing the guitar. Her next endeavor will most likely be photography.

Answers

page 11—640 cm^3

page 17—C = 43.96 cm; C = 69.08 in.

page 21—720°; 1080°; 180°; 90°

page 29—B. a planter that is 24 inches tall and 36 inches long

page 39—approximately 2 pounds, 10 ounces; 127 pounds, 6 ounces